Carnival Cocoon

Poetry Collection

DOW
DOMEST

TAX CUT

JUST SAY NO
TO THE
GLAMOROUS LI

ALPACA

Carnival Cocoon

Poetry Collection

Featuring poems from

Carnival Cocoon

the album

For my father Dave,
my mother Karen,
my sister Debbie,
and my niece Kelsey

Published by Scottie Miller Music LLC
Minneapolis, MN
scottiemiller.com

Published in the United States of America

ISBN 979-8-9864834-0-5 (paperback) ~ ISBN 979-8-9864834-1-2 (ebook)

Library of Congress Control Number: 2022913059

First printing August 2022

Cover and interior design
Lynn Phelps

Cover and chapter illustrations
William Phelps

Photograph on page 83, cover and chapter V. reference photos
Jim Vasquez

Photograph location for poster wall and Ferris wheel
Betty Danger's, Minneapolis, Minnesota

Printing and Binding
Bolger Press Inc.
Minneapolis, Minnesota

Acknowledgments

The Poems

For Pamela, without whom I would have never ventured the risk to sift through hundreds upon hundreds of poems, nor pursued the concept of improvising piano underneath. Your creativity, reassurance and inspiration gave me the strength to reach for a level of vulnerability I've never felt. You helped me nourish a deeper form of expression that has become one of the most liberating projects I've ever taken on.

My sincere thanks to editor/author Candelin Wahl, for helping articulate my artistic vision in this collection, and to Mud Season Review based in Burlington, Vermont, who led me into her capable hands.

Endless thanks to my creative team: Lynn Phelps at Phelps Design, illustrator William Phelps and photographer Jim Vasquez.

Thank you Nici Lawson Website Design for helping create an easy way to watch, listen and read.

My personal thanks to Peter Burke, Steve Nelson, Denby Auble, Daria Kelly, Sara King and Rhonda James for your unconditional support and guidance. To my SMB brothers, Dik Shopteau, Patrick Allen and Mark O'Day, for your continued support and vibrant friendship on and off the stage.

My love and gratitude to Ruthie Foster and the band: Ruthie, Larry Fulcher, Brannen Temple, Hadden Sayers and our team, Kasi Greathouse and Jennifer Salem. Each of you helped me maintain inspiration and focus with this project, reminding me of the blessing we share in self-expression through music and art.

The Album

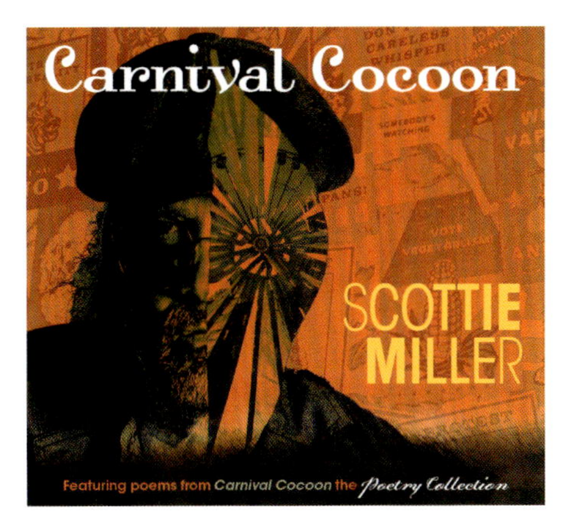

Carnival Cocoon
SCOTTIE
MILLER
Featuring poems from Carnival Cocoon the Poetry Collection

Since the inception of this project and my first public performance of "Ah, New York" on the Legendary Rhythm & Blues Cruise, Peggy Lou at WWOZ New Orleans has been airing demos of these pieces on her spoken word radio show, *Awake and Willing.* To you my friend, merci beaucoup. "Insanity is the playground of the unimaginative!"

My sincere gratitude to violinist/cellist Cierra Alise Hill, for your flawless and organic interpretations of these compositions in live performance and the studio. Thank you for your insight and mindfulness with the improvisational nature of this music and spoken/sung word.

Special thanks to those who attended our "Poetry/Piano" prerelease performances in the Twin Cities. Because of you and the support of venues like the Dunsmore Jazz Room at Crooners, the 318 Cafe and Lakeshore Players Theater, I found the freedom and the stages to explore this creation during a global pandemic and at a time of great unrest in our community and in our world.

It takes a village to tune a village, and to bring a project of this size to life. My soul is filled with gratitude to the extraordinary musicians who helped me set 23 of these poems and stories to music on the album version of *Carnival Cocoon:*

Cierra Alise Hill - *Violin, Cello*
Bex Gaunt - *Violin*
Jesse Kellermann - *Viola*
Greg Byers - *Cello, Double Bass*
JT Bates - *Drums and Percussion*
Jeff Bailey - *Double and Electric Bass*

Strings arranged by Cierra Alise Hill.
Ruthie Foster - *Vocals* on "Stay."
(Ruthie appears courtesy of Blue Corn Records.)

Recorded, mixed and mastered by Steve Kaul at Wild Sound Studio in Minneapolis.

My sincere thanks to Steve Kaul and the Kaul family. Your passionate, calm spirit and experience brought us safely across great mountains of notes, oceans of sound and genre-bending creation.

Download here, at your favorite online music retailer or at scottiemiller.com

I. Walking on Eggs

II. The Gibbous Moon

◉ On CD

III. Beggar, Banker, Fisherman Pay

IV. This Love Is Found in Shadows

V. 24 Hours in Mexico

I.

Walking on Eggs

Walking on Eggs

You see
anxiety
          for lengthy periods,
(like all your life)
erodes
      your
  nerves.

One wonders if it's adrenaline
but quickly discovers the truth.
Tracing steps
to youth—
locked in outhouses,
green twig in the latch.

Busy bus rides
downtown
in the slippery
January snow.
The old man who used to call me whippersnapper,
I liked that guy.

Long trip home,
so many stops,
melodies of Chick
soaring through my head—
the music I was fed,
the life I've led,
the sunken warp
to my bed.

Infinite melodies
scroll in atoms
that bounce
  between
    my
  eyes—
when I close them
only fragments
that float
above the drowning rivers
of that tenuous time

when all the drugs in town
pressed
against my mind—
  unkind
in post, really.

Ratcheted, rusted
bolts and joints
seize and hack,
as memory points
          back—wards
to early days.

When nights too late
startled the sun,
          screwdriver gun—
fruit juice
   citrus
         burned.
Slept through first-hour history again,
just 'cuz you're paranoid doesn't mean they're not out to get ya'.

Then the law came asking questions—sent out to the farm
where the man
had me rooting
through beehives in barns—
          nails through my shoe,
            snakes off my cuffs,
          bridled my fear
                              with those 13-year-old puffs.

          Tensing my belly,
rocking my legs,
          lost out on Shelly
I'm still walking on eggs.

Berklee

I.
There's that wet again—
socked in and sopped up
on Boylston and Mass. Ave
as the depressive get depresser'ed
in that all-day work—
on them pianers'
on them drum pads
on them horns!

Find me a soundproof room,
I'll give you a stab at Donna Lee,
a crack at "Ornithology"
"Here's That Rainy Day"—
coming down in torrents on
furrowed young brows.

Bony wrists
swollen digits
sore paws
empty bellies,
hands peeling
from drinking that dirty
dorm-room water—
come up from that
janky old
brothel plumbing,
from that stanky old Charles.

Probably still some TB
on them bunks,
or some cheap copper bracelet
found in a lump
beneath the dump
    heap
miles beneath—
years beneath—
    In Miles we believe!

Ghosts left there lingering,
bewildered
in those studious clouds of education
that hover
in the November rains
of Boston.

Pulsating vaults
leaking notes
tears
death
epiphanies—
sauntering through the New England winter.

2.
I miss home and Thanksgiving in '86,
but a slice of pepperoni from Gino's will do just fine.
Gives real good grease—
tip that pie
let it drain,
but not too much
that's where the flavor lies.
Drizzles on that triple-thick paper plate—
loaded up
with cheap little napkins
to sop it all up—
            stains my knuckles.

The buzz-hum
drum-steps
rattle—
para-diddling
rain drops
in truncated rhythms
            bounce
against my eyes.

I can hear
some collusion
between a dozen or more
quadrupled, quintupled
rhythms.

Wooden shreds of sticks,
  dust and cigarette ash
            season the carpet.

3.
It's a Faneuil, Quincy Market rainy day
spent drying out in the lobby,

where the beautiful African singers
told me what a powerful aura
I have around my head.
Purple, they said,
 with amber,
           very strong.

O, the confidence came,
not from transcribing Shearing,
but from them ladies—
from their glowing,
butter-brown skin
  underneath their
  flaming dresses of yellow, gold and orange.

Soaked me in their
black-ink hair
wrapped in sky-blue buns.
Ugandan smiles,
tribal lineage
reflected in stars
from their ivory white teeth—
  reached into my chest,

           tickled my loneliness.

Pandemic - Riots MPLS

March 27, 2020

I.
Away we go
with all the noise and tank low hum—
emergency helicopters
          buzz
the frozen sky,
race across town to save a flipped wreck.
Some tragedy-stricken guy
bleeding out,
          warm
at 2 degrees F.

Whizzing high pressure
singes the Minnesota night
with a vengeance.
  It culls the weakened souls.

Even I have seen
death
at least three times
in this polar vortex
of whipping trails.

Smacked facedown in the gutter
in a foot of slush—
flying high, airborne in a Honda Prelude
with a tux and a briefcase
          levitated,
sliced near-through
          windshield
by an exit sign.
Overdosed, too much blow
where the snow
swallowed up
whole,
all at once.
Stuffed up
          nose.

S h a k e ' s y o u r lips.

Even I have drawn
narrow
the arteries of my brain
with the million dollar
re-uptake inhibitor,
shortened the synapses,
shrunk the think
            to think—
dulling the morbid,
depressing ideology,
ramping up quelled euphoria.
Exploding fantasy,
instinct in command,
youthful assumption,
        longing—
                    receiving.

2.
Swiss Alps desire
boils the pot.
Living through death,
healing the rot.
Pills back up—
pharmacies fill
            the never ending
                    void.

Watch out for what's not being
numbed,
dumbed,
thumbed down—
           all you forgot
           will come back around—

to live,
 love—
       breathe.

Space Heaters and Cocoa

Eggs and waffles
drifting shaloffles
plink, blip, crat'
creaking house—
plaster s-h-i-v-e-r-s—
          impending wrath of winter.

Space heaters and cocoa—
should be comforting,
but I'm gratefully depressed
          by the necessity.

Tainted heroine
frozen gypsies—
fentanyl deluge
skiing the luge—
slide, thwark'
jaggly' pounce.

The cat's in the hamper again

               the ashtray's overflowing.

The Gritty Border

He rambled down the road like a riddle unsolved
He spent 15 years inside a 12-foot stall
It was the wrong time for the crime—
There's that two-dollar phone call
They said would only cost him a dime

He's the man with his life on a long, thin line
The one in chains with a long-term fine
All he ever did was just sell a little bit
But he loved all that money and he just couldn't quit

Tipping back and forth across the gritty border
Chipping away at all that brick and mortar
Was only a matter of time before it all came down
It was a'bound to happen, he was a'sure to be found

Caught up in a pace
You can tell by the lines on his face—
He was a'hangin' in a lane that went way too fast
But in the back of his mind he knew it—just wouldn't last

Now so many years are gone
His wife and kids have moved on—
Faint mem'ry of who daddy used to be
Barbed wire horizon's all they'll ever see

You know it's all wrong—it's all wrong
He's caught up in a broken system
He keeps tryin' to stay strong—
But the law doesn't listen

and you see a young man turn old
before his time.

Stay

You ever been wound up so tight
You can't think straight, you can't think right?
Unsure about the future
And everything's so unsure

No tape left to rewind
And everybody's so unkind
Too much time in your hands
So hard to make new plans

Stay, just stay
Don't let it turn you out
Don't you believe in the doubt
Stay, just stay
Don't let it get you down
'Cuz we need you around

You can't find any justice
I keep lookin' but it's just us
Too long in the trench
Bad judge on the bench

More money, more greed, more power
Big guns shootin' down from a tower
No wonder people wanna give up
But we know when enough is enough

There's never been a better reason not to give up
You really mean somethin' and we need ya'
I see your value; I see your worth
It's been a part of you since your birth

When this world tries to tear you down
Stand up and rebuild your town
The same one where both you and I live
We see you, and everything you give.

Whiskey, Coffee

1.
Deli ham with lots of cheese
sopping cakes in pools of maple—
butter piled high on the plate.

Chevy Chevette
run through the ice
rolled
like a tiny submarine.
Broken knee
rusty crutches—
was a long, slushy
limp home.

Whiskey, coffee
whiskey, coffee
warm and numb,
            alert and dumb.

Pounding rhythms
  bounce the car—
wet kiss
the goodbye nudge.
Off to Boston—
see you again
my second chair love.

Charles River's
current-sludge
laid out Sundays
on the grass—
brains overloading
smiles exploding
sex imploding.

Stone table chess
the brilliant few
amidst the spitting
yelling, aching men—
            stiff and wounded.

2.
Paper bags
shattered pints
scattered on the curb.
Sewer gas in rising steam
carried through
Harvard Square.

Whiskey, coffee
whiskey, coffee—
        burns the salty lips.

Can't trust the Real Book guy
and the dense rain will hold you in.

Broken upright strings that
            snap
the pant leg—
            chilling shock.
Impatient cigarettes
burn another notch.

Dissecting sounds—
creeping slowly
        down
hallways of endless pianos.

High School Wrestling

This life has got me pinned down
like a high school wrestler on a sweaty, stinky-ass floor mat.
It's got me wet-towel beaten in a junior high locker room—
licked and locked down—
inked and printed—
they threw away the key.
There ain't no solace for me.

I'm not unique or some special case,
I'm well aware of despair in this place.
I've done it or seen it, but I'm haunted by lies
    that well up and fuck with my dreams at night.

My memory is tainted, so often inaccurate,
such that these lies aren't even true.
Obscured by the fog of old addictions,
the truth is—I've lost my way through.

Not much capacity?
    I don't think so.

Not very brave?
    Proven that wrong.
Send me a heart attack, I'll laugh through the pain,
my eyes have seen floods that are empty of rain.

Troubadour, wordsmith, creative junkie
with no solid ground to lay my discovery.
An ample, learned and helpful citizen,
in a world I'm not sure I know how to live in.

Now with my penchant for classical music,
        smoothing the cracks in my so fitful mind—
    Never afraid of a road that's too slick,
            regardless of what I might find.

A Better Way to Cope

There is magic floating through the air tonight,
in a new dimension.
Allows a gleaming light to shine,
and it smells of less contention.

While greed pushes on
from white houses up on a hill,
another show of muscle,
while Jenny swallows down another pill.

I'm just tryin' to stay above the fray,
but the years add to my pot.
There are gold and diamonds piling up,
but I've no need for more than what I've got.

I don't want to be the one
who gives up on his hope.
If you can tell me how you do it,
maybe I can find a better way to cope.

I saw the buses leave the city,
and crowds gather on the street.
We're sick and tired of all the trouble,
while the peace is crumbling at our feet.

Truth and justice
are knocking at the door.
As the day comes to a close,
there is the hope of something more.

I suppose we've all been fighting now,
for thousands of years.
But that doesn't change the fact,
there's still salt burning in our tears.

Will there be another chance
after all the damage done?
Will the man out on the street
even get to see another setting sun?

I think I'll drive on down to St Louis
and see my friends out there.
Get right-sized with the notion,
that all in love and war isn't fair.

I don't want to be the one
who gives up on his hope.
If you can tell me how you do it, man,
maybe I can find a better way to cope.

If you can tell me how you do it,
maybe I can find a better way to cope.

II.

The Gibbous Moon

Conjunction

The night blew a kiss
to part the day's clouds
revealing Saturn
in its conjunction with Jupiter.

How sweet a marriage
of opposing attraction
as wisdom and order
are confused by innocent play—

Teacher watches over the twins at recess—
as Sirius shimmers
in pearlescent wonder.

Fire on the Bayou

Have you seen the bayou near Pontchartrain,
her tangled tributaries
draped in Spanish moss?

She is ablaze.

Water soaked in soil—
eternities of brackish oil,
cleansing herself in regrowth
time and time again.

She is ablaze.

Sparkling embers stick like tar
to her cypress knees and snarled brush.
Ancient alligators young and old
scurry from their nests
to middle water—
dark and muddy, murky water
filled with vine, mulch and fodder.
Have you seen it?

She is ablaze—
renewing herself.

Precious, haunting bayou—
the spider's matrix, year-old web
singed by licking flames and heat—
dampened, yet she burns with might,
strange how water burns through night.

Fleeing egret, hanging snakes
rush to find the safest place—
silenced hum the crickets muted.
Heartwood smolders
in burnt-orange hues.

She is ablaze.

Flakes of ash rest upon the backs
of a throng of giants.
Unharmed, sensing the heat
upon their riveted scales—
eyes simmer beneath the crackling liquid,
biding their time
as Hestia finishes her reparation.

The tender, humble king of the swamp
survives to tell the tale.
Have you seen the bayou?

She is ablaze.

The Greedy Shore

The greedy shore lurks,
her appetite unsated.
Brave men on ships she tracks,
her belly ever baiting.

No truth in sea, or beguiling skies,
the winter wrecks, the bodies claimed.
Windswept echoes carry the cries
of men enshrined to liquid fame.

They tried their hand at sailing through
the clever course was still in sight.
Reefing, tacking, then heaving-to,
the day swam into night.

No worse a turn for jaded men
to see themselves turned blue
by winds amid the fickle ocean,
lost stories of that prideful crew.

Port Fairy dresses up its waves,
they glimmer metal reflections.
Australian ghosts know each they saved
and all who reached the heavens.

No Trace

Full-breasted sails and stoutly hull,
chased through waves of concrete sea.
Ahead lay the endless, restless course,
before us lay our destiny.

A catch we've only dreamed to find,
if God should grant our take—
atop the waters which may allow
safe passage to calm our wake.

Rocking wind and jagged coral,
how did we ever get so shallow?
The devil found his toy to fondle,
a drink from which to swallow.

He came from stern and wayward port,
mixing and jumbling, frothing fright.
No rudder held, nor direction told,
the Dark One showed his face that night.

The tearing surf and wicked hand
of whom I dare not fathom,
had its grip upon this ship
and sent us to his chasm.

Gone.

Lost.

No trace.

Risen

Still on the fast flip
moon in the full
chest wrapped with irons
clattering,

shatter in the windless night.

Glimpse of the new phase
no need to rush
face falling down
glowing,

blinking, sensitive to light.

A leaf tumbles,
strips the vine
stares at earth
vacant,

long the constant, suffering grind.

Lifts the rock
and with it the weight
illuminates worth
risen—

driftwood appears in the current.

If Only the Soft Wind Would Blow

It was here, now it's gone—
if only its warmth would brush my face
I would swallow it down, taste its sweet grape on my tongue

Ever adoring—rushing, whipped
and luscious sound
trickles through my ears

In every waking moment I wait for its return—
the sky-kissed breeze of a northern night
to spin me 'round and swoon my head to confident center

Sky to earth and space to heart
let it come again I pray—
        I feel lost without the soft wind's grace

Neglect all else to wait for her, and sense the coming winter slur
        slide through wretched muck and goo, the slush and ice have run me through

        O great north country, vast and clean—
        resentful, bitter the winter's theft
        of soft-spring summer winds that blew
        by March I think you've made it true!

        Nowhere to find the soft wind blow,
                                        yet set my hopes on the melting snow.

Silver Sky

So grand the silver sky
with clouds dispersed like feathers.
Same in me this whirling heart,
and tense to this I'm tethered.

Charred and thick a storm may settle,
my wrists are taut and sore.
The search is on through sage and amber
to find my peaceful lore.

That language spoken—deaf I seem—
must break a rotted beam.
Above my head no screeching hawk
to help me find a fresher stream.

Black, the hue and dampened blue
my eyes take dust and crack.
Too many of my nerves been broken—
thank God she gave me slack.

The polar breeze of cooling Canada
sits above the border sly—
she trickles in slow at first in fall
by December she's a frozen cry.

Bemoans my final words,
depletes my endless purge—
not alone with the rifle shell,
or the sulfur powder and that stark old smell.

That which comes now day or night,
it will melt the wax to wick—
there could be age and damage done,
so pray that time is quick.

To think we're not the only ones—
not a fish or just one wave
of frothing, soapy suds and surf
from Port Fairy's protected bays.

Mourning Dove

Quiet whisper mourning dove—
        coo

Gentle perch mourning dove—
        coo

Stare unabated at the sky above
for hawk and falcon shadows.
We need your perseverance dove,
your stable grounded coo.

Angels within you mourning dove
remain strong and drenched with love.
No harm or danger find their way
to ruffle your downy cloak.

        Taking down your heartbeat slow,
        until sunken calm is all you know.

The Howling Dark

Frequent rolls, a heavy rain,
dragons drenched, the fires dowsed.
Stinging bolts of lightning pain,
villagers flee their unsafe house.

Calamity floods the sandy shores,
roaring mud fills crowded streets.
Ships tossed, lost their moors,
angry gods—their furious fleets.

Who finally comes to stop the shred?
We're beyond the point of gaining trust.
The fabric weakened by evil men,
no blessed mercy left for us.

Still we search the skies for angels
who might come back to halt the pillage.
Yet not in sight, hope fades and dangles,
the flattened earth has lost all knowledge.

To counter fear through humility,
we bind ourselves to the strongest tree—
though fiery winds may scorch the bark,
we shall not shrink from the howling dark.

Mother Dunia

Never has the Earth seen such deep pain—
hurts in her roots, deep down in her veins.
Corroded, infected a rust-bloodied red,
as tortured vessels sail in her stead.

Gone are the days when saviors come
to rescue her from tides and receding shores.
Lost are the chances from innocent days
to reap clean fruit from the trees she bore.

Sad as the day Antigonus fell,
and sorrow befell the people of Phrygia.
Victories won—battles lost,
leaves none good for the finding—
each bear a senseless lust imbibing.

Greed and progress grow the cancer
within us all, the same earthly injury.

Let low cello play with pedal point!
Let low pitch on piano nod
her luminous head to God,
that all be halted for her sake!

That all things fail to stop the whirl
of busy beehive and should honey give,
let drip thick sugar and pollinate all,
so few are the seeds that take their fall.

A single tear of rain tickled the back of my shoulder.

I heard a faint whimper,
the dry soil cracking—
I felt Mother's temper,
her patience lacking.

The Gibbous Moon

has finally come—
the light has bent
and not too soon.

Old prayers are told,
sung in tune
with all the scattered
wandering souls—
who lay in peace
from restless doom,
and ease their minds
in lesser tolls.

O Sacred Night

A foxhole prayer in the face of threat
when nothing could reduce my debt

A single feather floating, crumbling
mixed with ash and dirt, fumbling—
until it reached into my soul
I saw no rice within my bowl

Yet forth the coming day I rise
receiving grace with no disguise

O sacred night
you touch me
With warm embrace
you heal me

From where I walked an icy path
you've steered me blind and eased the wrath

Showed mercy when I begged in pain
and cried out, not knowing your name

How should it be you grant me this?
How can the weight of burdens lift
from such a heavy load of dread
and all I've conjured in my head?

Listen to the cracking thunder
squint your eyes and blur the stars

Ever will the crop sow under
seeds of God grow where you are.

all are welcome

FREE to STAY

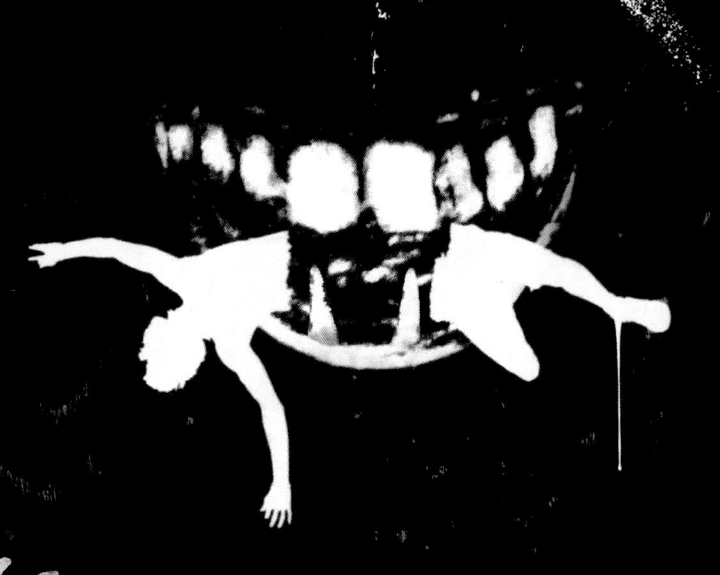

III.

Beggar, Banker, Fisherman Day

Minstrel, Monster, Alchemist

Through blinding, wringing walls of rain, I'll sing and play this song
No words shall slip from my tongue, or sit on earth too long
No wretched surf or grounded bird will wrack me from the quest
The diamond shard within the wood, revealed this naked chest.

Fruits that fill the air and space—the melodies abound
Gravel voice and blasting horn entwine the rapturous sound
Takers, givers, lovers all lay gathered on the rock
Shouting, slanderous racist ears too deaf to join the flock.

The rocks that hold my native land in softened womb they lay
'Long the frozen miles of mint-crisp seas along the bay
Fields of barley, golden rich I taste the river's lead
Upon the wheat of Sami-Mark we sew the finest thread.

Minstrel, monster, alchemist I dare to work the night
This brave and tempted body how it runs with fight or flight
Old friend the night has stared me down and brought me to my knees
The day will come when all old men find chance their maker's please.

I Rode Upon the Bareback Quarter

She felt my nerves
And with them twitched
Her hoofs etched mud like heavy mortar
We flew to the distant, risky border
Into the reins of time we were stitched.

Only when her gait ran steady
Was I lifted out of earthly realms
Where heavens start and souls are ready
Empty of their sinful felony
Appraised by only honest helms.

Peace rose from the foggy earth
A clear and drying sun appeared
To help this tired and broken birth
Be placed once more on the holy hearth
At the feet of a gracious God not feared.

Beggar, Banker, Fisherman Pay

Southern winds blow through the port,
give rest to northern chills.
Hold fast the breath of winter's snort
that test longshoremen's skills.

Frozen still the river's brunt
as ice shards clog the way to shore.
Stranded fish, their gills will grunt—
stuck, and spring may come no more.

'Long the shore stand wives in waiting—
their old men with grizzly hands.
Scuffed and wet their boots are draining—
salt and sea crumble in the sand.

Wobbly sea legs steady themselves
then walk inside warm tavern halls—
candle, pipe, a pint on the shelf
for two rejoined where safety calls.

Then latent merriment tires thee
from long the journey's hours spent.
Slow the catch and short the tally,
credit given or a dollar lent.

All are welcome and free to stay,
not one left out on this cold night—
beggar, banker, fisherman pay,
no mind their purse albeit light.

The Farmer's Wife

Wood to chop,
husband's gone
living on her own.

Farmer's wife who's lost it all,
her face has never shown.

Running, whipping reckless cat,
skinny in the barn,
winter's blotchy tangled nap,
horses stomp the yarn.

Cold, the endless winter wrath,
frozen tears that crack,
days that break the hardened path
caked upon her back.

Ever common times have come,
stirs the idle hands,
breaking ropes and knots undone,
can she make a stand?

Harvest in the face of luck,
planted in the field,
just as kind the killer's gun,
never does it yield.

Flirting with Darkness

Sometimes I marvel at the company I keep
Much too good for this messed-up heap
Been to the ground with my chin on the curb
shaken—
disturbed.

Somehow with age I seem less than I'm worth
The years like worn tires and a belly of girth
Too many cigarettes, and way too much pie
The dope doesn't cut it,
less sight from my eye.

Drank more than my share and no matter the time
I've wasted hours on whiskey and wine
All while my friends tried to reel me in close
The further I strayed, the more random the prose.

Flirting with darkness, dancing with ghosts
Solving world issues with blow on my nose
Truth in the morning, trembling in sweat
One look in the mirror,
I'm filled with regret.

Three Past Lives

1.
Slanted arrow cut quick through the air,
Then landed a step from us just over there.
No time to think or move from the path,
The wind from the east saved us both from its wrath.
Stepping were we upon cold, sacred ground,
Where no man or woman should ever be found.
Steer clear if it takes you an extra three days,
Or risk being buried your ashes there lay—

Your spirit entombed.

2.
Brash north winds, cut slivers on cheeks,
Blinded by snow through which no light could leak.
Turning in circles, no path and beguiled,
Stop, rest and breathe lest we fall to the wild.
Damp was the smoldering fire we built,
To save us from losing the life that we filled.
Never seen such a dark night of still,
How frozen our hands in that fragmented chill—

Broken to pieces.

3.
She stood with her face to the soft morning sun,
I arose to the sight as her prayers had begun.
Flashed through my mind what a war we have lost,
Yet dying was I from the bullets' steep cost.
You must go on, I think I'll stay here,
I've lost too much blood, yet there's nothing to fear.
We've both lived it once and we'll live it again,
Next time I'll learn not to break but to bend—

Then ease our passage.

Yin and Yang

The empath heals and lives,
While the greedy sink their teeth
Into the flesh of the vulnerable,
Remorseless of the wounds.

The pusher never gives,
The taker sits beneath—
Ready to lunge, take any and all
Regardless of his doom.

Depending on which side you sit,
It matters not if you can see.
The blindness darkens both the lights
Of hope and hate, the yin and yang.

Temperance or intolerance
Water or searing fire—
My ocean and your country
Mingle in the loss of civility.

Leveling the imbalance
Squelched by desire—
The charred roots of a new tree
Collapse in front of whose eyes can see.

The only difference in you or me is a restless ancient melody
Patiently waiting for us to open the door,

As we all yearn for something more.

Division

Straining to hope
wandering souls
absent memory
buried in holes

Tempted by trust
in leaders of men
crumbling to rust
failed us again

Captured by anger
locked up by hate
families in need
turned down at the gate

Pulling apart
fine threads of peace
tearing the fabric
of all we believe

Days have passed
when fascists reigned—
so why the craving
to feel that again?

Goddess of the Wereth Eleven

She is brave and burrows deep
within the risk—
surrounding fear
layered carapace
muting gasps
before the fall.

Lends her pure
blue oxygen
filtered wind—
washing fields
of moldy blood
cleansing war
from insidious
tyrannical ramblings.

Decomposes
        the rusted shell.

Hears the dreams
        they couldn't tell.

For Belgium

*22 March 2016**

The air is tight
new smoke, fog rising
legs cut, blood scratched
hatred's fury shown in doggerel face

short breathing
from beloved Belgium
in Hell's cauldron
this Tuesday morning.

Where is kindness
Where are the gods
Where is peace

or love's reaching?
of life's pure vengeance?
of young hearts longing?

Pungent breezes come
from dark faces' wrath
blood soaked with gnashing teeth
peace defeated, black reddened

by wafting stench
no longer arid
as rage has won
washed upon jagged shores.

Simple and true
lost in the queue
Cannot tempest come
Cannot she blow clean

the good deeds of Saint Amalberga
missing their finding.
and rinse all away?
all madness and fray?

Trumpets gold blasting
forte and accent
bell of trombone
resolve with French horn
riveting drums march there
turn all toward the sound

Heaven's sonata
thunderous drum
shake earth to its begging
lull to soft calming
to startle attention
come forth to the pounding!

Voyage of thieves
murderous scoundrels
kings and queens
gone is the kingdom

arrived with deceit
plundered and pilfered
erased from their throne
where kindness once roamed.

**On the morning of 22 March 2016, three coordinated suicide bombings occurred in Belgium: two at Brussels Airport in Zaventem, and one at Maalbeek metro station in central Brussels. Thirty-two civilians and three perpetrators were killed; more than 300 people were injured.*

How Can the Poor Man Ever Win?

Dogs are nipping at his heels
calf is bleeding, he's got two flat wheels
pedals knocking, bruised his shin
and that damn dog just won't let him win

Rattling lines in the squirming town
fighting thugs and wondering how—
that box is so small it taunts his rest
and that raspy cough just won't clear in his chest

His wringing heart and his ringing ears
dry and caked, then soaked by his own tears
the gods move days and nights in caves
it's a random choice in the lives they save

Oh so bleak the dark, and weak the soul
a troll stands stifling every goal—
there's a tariff to cross the bridge,
lest you drown, or get stuck by a plunderer's shiv

Those who pillage to get their take
they jostle and jolt 'til their ankles break—
seeps from their eyes a most hideous soot
the same that trample the weakest root—

Of men and women with scant, bare thread
or the many with minds that are seen as dead—
there is rain without a lifting cloud
it pounds the soil, encourages the proud

Burnt, scorned, judged and done
conscienceless, mindless of those they shun
they're working, they're seething, they're absent and thin
the rich will win with a prideful sin—

and I ask you

how can the poor man

ever win?

IV.

This Love Is Found in Shadows

Goodnight Sweet, Tender Light of Dawn

Lay down in groves of chamomile—
Let slumber take your every breath
And wander with you in the depth
In waters-wading, puddles, ponds
Layered pearl-winged, silent swan
Drift from shore to deepening song
Where lays the lasting melody strong.

Illuminate brilliant hues
Of amber, gold and violet rays—
Let not your hand or shoulder raise
In anger never eyes shall gaze
With you it's simple, easy talk
And down forgiving paths we walk
No need for refuge when you're near
It seems you're never far from here.

She Saved Him from His Dreams

He yearned for youth
discovered truth
his aging shell
had more to tell
of love's sweet words
upon his tongue
that might be heard
by welcome ears—
or vibrant embrace
might be held
by arms waiting

where colors meld.

In Unison

The blowing wind of connection
seamlessly bears the fruits
of our love—
the linkage to each other

We are blues, we are heart—
West Coast troubadours
East Coast junkies
Midwest freeze-outs
southern hospitalities

Dirty, worn
clean, unsworn
reckless beauties, asleep backstage—
confess your quiet thoughts
soak up every missing ounce
rub your skin on kindred hands—
together we can change
this slanted world.

China in Paris

Stepped lightly, China in Paris—
carefully tended each of us
with sweet wines and warm coffee,
wasn't the drink attracted me.

Working the room, welcoming all,
shadow six feet, man she's tall!
Graceful dance from green room to bar,
I wished her feet moved more like tar.

Off to smoke, to see her again,
passed the bar—she leaned on her chin.
This tour should stop for her I see,
two more nights would satisfy me.

Long ways from home while in her town,
a canceled flight might keep me around.
Just a chance to see if she might
take one stroll under dim street light—
one minute, away from the noise
from the concert where we were poised.

Her eyes were dark espresso,
lean her arms and stretched her torso.
Deep my longing-heart's desire,
singed by flames that never tire.

I do admit I played each note
wishing they'd reach her ears and float.
No time to speak in common word,
my stay was brief as a restless bird.

Create a longer piece to play?
Somehow turn fate my way?

Sumptuous Wind

A haunting wind
in the grove of night
enveloped my ears
while the whirling of my torment lingered.
Even during my most confused thoughts,
        she came.

Sumptuous wind
with her silky, liquid dance—
coated the grass
        in filtered drizzle,
distracted me
long enough
                        to catch my breath.

Golden Honey

Tickled by lust
 desire abounds
Natural thirst
 quenched by the sounds
Golden honey
 drips from her lips—
Her lulling voice
 in timbres of bliss.

Windswept

She'll come to you in dreams of wonder;
she'll come to you in waking day.
She rides above the roaring thunder,
where we step and where we lay.

Upon the tempest winds she soars;
her arms unveil her widening pennons—
ascends and guards exhaustive shores,
sings of unknown legends.

May you only bear the load you can,
and believe the place you are is true—
for come the day when all your plans
no longer bind or serve you.

There will be a raining on my heart

to drench the dehydrated sands of my soul—
creating new life in me,
born of a blue and gentle sleep—
She'll be there.

A wayward wind from a Himalayan crest
found its way across the world
and rested on my back—
She floats there.

It comes on the sound of rushing rivers
washing on the eroded shores of my being—
She's resting there.

I left her there long ago, to rest her weary head
upon a precipice of safety from the storm.
Her strength regained she's calling now,
her love again is born.
I feel it in my aching bones
through winter's long abuse.
Her mooring and its tie to me
can never be cut loose.

Love goes astray, the heart will pay
a heavy toll to take—
no benefactors of this fleeting wealth
or hearts lost longing.

It matters not from where love came
or where it ends up.
She is not meant to be found.
She's not intended to be arrived upon,
She is free.

She cannot be tethered by our own ignorant will,
she will come and conquer you when you feel content.
She will have her way with you as she pleases—
the way will be full, or it may be sparing.
It may not show every face in the mirror of your wondering,
therefore, hope—

Hope, wish, pray and give thanks
for such an untainted thing as love!
Not ruined by our own understanding,
not stifled by human oppression,
unbound by rule or demanding—
a gift, not a possession.

This Love Is Found in Shadows

Love that floods the dreary plains,
fills the shallow crevice.
Pouring, drenching, soothing love,
from souls of deepest longing.

Empath, giver, wonder light,
exposes withered grief.
Shining, glimmering rays of white
reform the common thief.

This love is found in shadows:
in the damp and rotting cloth
worn by travelers, gypsies lost
in nations gripped by tyranny.

Love embodies—*sings!*
Spreads her wings and coddles earth.
Resting rapid, anxious hearts—
brings them back to birth.

Hu Jun Di Painting

She moves like stirring winds,
graceful and bold.
Her lips on canvas blush—
the harsh seasons have no effect,
nor age her porcelain cheeks.

Deep, sable hair
soaked in painter's ink.
Dampened feather
draped
  across her breast.

The fox and wolf have laid the path
assured the way
  with every step—
dense, forest canopy
blots the guiding sun,
the hawk her flying eyes.

Her soul retains humility,
she summons the gods.

An unfurling leaf,
her love awaits the dawn—
            humble and quiet.

If her heart should find its mate
so shall the skies be full
            the rivers deep and cool
                        the air rich with breath.

            The earth warms her bare feet to touch
                        as she waits in tender sadness.

Never Seen the Snow Fall Quite This Hard

Wrinkled, stuffed and broken down
my tainted tongue will swallow
afterthoughts of joy and suffering
pounding heart will follow—
lurching, waning stilts of legs
standing toward tomorrow

You, uncertain recluse—
paint the color
close the door
mind your mother—
  teardrop tinged
your mind will bother
only when the nightfall
                                        flutters

Sense of sky is with us still—
deep the breath
of frigid lungful
            Tree bark cracks
    in clear-night chill
                                        silence in the vastness of stars

Chilled by months of bothersome cold
frozen ground below me scolds
rinse my hands in blessed streams
I speak your name in soft flute strains

My love, my blood, I call in dreams
Fair-faced liquid eyes, gaze into me!

        So I may sleep

                                        a peaceful

                                                            slumber.

NE Lowry Av

24 Hours in Mexico

Ah, New York

There on the street lies the gum spat out by every New Yorker and tourist
along the sidewalk of every corner, of every street and avenue.
Dried like some spotted Dalmatian in patterns of polka dots—
sorry sots.

There in the air just under your nose drifts the smell of a million hot dogs,
dumpsters, cardboard, dead rat, delicious Thai food, arid coffee bistro,
marinara red sauce, pasta, tacos—
ah, New York.

Horn honky, dragged-out junkie, broken-down jazzer, burnt-out rocker,
high-flying trader, hustling model, trust fund board skater, unhappy waiter.
All of us, swirling in a pot of steamed soup—
steamed soup.

Dishing it out for ten dollars a scoop.
Smiling or discerning, doesn't matter the look,
all are equal and the mayor's a crook—
toity art museum tourist book.

So flame on drag queens, burn your light bright, you're outta sight.
Sing on subway shouter,
fill your bucket high with bills!
"Keep the change cheapskate...cash only."

Blow your horn, move your mime,
paint your face, bring shoes to shine—
make the bed and freshen the room,
all are welcome in the carnival cocoon.

1800 Chicago Avenue

1.

Reckless Rudy and toothless Tootie,
each had their own little quirks.
Smiling, calling, shouting angrily
at all who walked by and offered no change,
no cup of coffee, no snort of whiskey—

It's only 7:30 AM outside the Bruegger's bagel shop on East Hennepin.
No cold wind seemed to dishevel them,
neither did the icy-sleet chipping at their barely clothed bodies—
too nuts to feel the burn or too stoned to see the turn.

Ahead at the light, the right turn yield,
the racing cars and hype—
important businessmen and -women might pause
for a well-dressed man to cross,
but not for Rudy or Tootie.
Just ram on through and maybe nick their shoe,
or knock their knee on the bumper of your shitty Mercedes.

Greedy, selfish.
Who cares anyway? They're just a couple of homeless drunks,
gacked outa their minds.
Hell they're better off dead anyway.
I'm late for work, can't you see, idiot!

Honnnnnk, long annoying startling
hooooonnnnnk!

Startling—*Heart jarrtlin'.*

2.

Off to the ER if the ambulance ever gets here.
Dog plasma, people plasma, which way do I go now? Which way do I go now?
Late and lazy them damned medics—
like that morning in Budapest
when that shooter fell and cracked his head wide open in front of me
on that mean old concrete—

Ah, let's just wait for the paddy wagon, and let them take him down to the drunk tank.
Bleeding head and brain damage likely—*"heeding bed and drain bramage."*
Just throw 'em in the back and see how long it takes.
Let's stop for coffee and eat some cakes.
Maybe he'll just die...
I ain't gonna cry...you?

3.
Enter 1800 Chicago and a bin full of addiction—
to rest, or not
with the DT-screaming recluses
all claiming to have someone else's name.

System's broke.

Grab your poke.

Smoke your smoke.

4.
The rich get richer, then kill their neighbor.
A lawyer gets them off by an elitist payer—
some large corporation to scatter the liability
between the lawyer and the judge with no attending jury.

The day will come when we all meet our maker—
the hopeless addict
the hopeless drunkard
the successful high financier
the banker's wife so dear—
the housewife
the veteran
the shady, kid-porn neighbor—
all dead,
all tuned for a reckoning—

or...nothing.

Global New Year's resolutions put off once again—

Hope and dread

Lucky to have a bed.

Bleecker Street

Drunken my friends a salty lot,
I used to fill many a pot.
Never tasted a moderate sum,
always in a state of dampened numb.

Barking dogs in a piss stench alley,
watching my back with pinpoint savvy.
Forging thoughts too many to count,
all to forget before they could mount.

Sober and clear as an ice shelf adrift,
letting it go, now I'm breathing a gift.
Unmerited peace every once in awhile,
reins me in close, reminds me to smile.

You know I'm a drunken salty sot,
and I'll never judge another man's plot.
Where men devote life in the warmth of a tavern,
soon shall I dry from my own misty cavern.

Surely we'll meet again somewhere on Bleecker—
never will my comrades have felt any weaker.
Yet if my friend starts to tremble and quiver,
my blanket I'll share on cold nights when they shiver.

I Wake to Many Melodies

I wake to many melodies
I wake to many melodies

Day and night have now become one
Soft wind with an icy nip
The house is warmed by the spring sun
My lips have not had a sip

I wake to many melodies

The patrons don't acknowledge me
For drink has not touched my tongue
My mouth speaks no apology
Still, girls with wine-stained hands come

I wake to many melodies

Black drapes won't block the morning sun
Too bright for a foggy head
To not disturb, she must have run
Her taxi spared me instead

Spared me from the dampened sheets
From where love has cooled, I rise—
A new day shines with tempered peace
What was the color of her eyes?

I wake to many melodies
I wake to many melodies.

Lowry Avenue Bridge

Lately there's been a bustling wind
blowing down Lowry Avenue—
whipping dried leaves, paper and napkins,
cigarette butts wick off the bridge.

Dropped into the Mississippi—
swirling current tosses debris and branches,
logs and rusty outboard boat motors—
swallowed up and sent to a dark,

mucky
depth.

Tickles the sumac and ferns along the shore—
wilt, weave dripping wet, they droop like an old man's neck.

Nighttime comes, sun fell and hid behind the earth—

Venus appears—

fish awaken—

The cycle of life continues
for the good, the bad, the indifferent,
the smooth, the rough, the overconfident.

The proud, ignorant or indignant.
All raise their hands in distress;
All pray with the same desperation—

To find a pleasurable sensation.

Fish and Rice

I stumble—
I gain speed, then I regress.

There's quicksand in my dreams—
I'm pushing to run, but I'm stuck in the mud.

Where is my peace?
Why do I scramble?
Directionless wind
Intermittent thunder!

Dense the fog so thick in my soul
that beckons to love and be released from its hold—
ringing in my ears, my muscles contract
it's a wonder my heart survived the attack.

It'll happen again, or a new aging predicament—
a harrowing leap off the Washington Bridge
where cars careen off the snow-laden ramp
that's never been plowed, and won't relieve the cramp
of the damp,
c-o-l-d

river—

the hard, wooden sliver—

each with a cut that'll *bite and make you shiver.*

[sung]
There are millions of people so cold to the greeting,
they look strangely at me while I'm eating...

Fish and rice.

Adrenalina

Depth charge in the soul, the benzo-booze bounce
Gave up my control, sentenced for an ounce
They can hold me in this pen until they wear me down so thin
That I can fit my mind through spaces, and change the world from within

Crunching at the seams, this mania's staying longer
I can't control these highs and my depression's gettin' stronger
If I don't numb it out real soon, I might just melt down from inside
Burning inner surge, someone find me a faster ride!

Born into this life, tryin' to purge an urge
Always felt it simmering, waitin' for the surge
An endless lust for danger, a constant chance of risk
Thirst for heavy drink, or a mind-numbing fix

Anything to quell this nervous inner fight
Tortured in the daytime, taunted through the night
Mingling here with demons, swimming there with fools
Good thing with demons is they never float in pools.

24 Hours in Mexico

I.
I came to Puerto Vallarta with long, curly hair and silk clothes,
a felt black cape and a mandolin.
I must have been out of my mind—
looking for something free and to roam the dark streets
where the restaurant hawkers yelled,
"Two for one all fucking night long! Two for one all fucking night long!"

I sat above and across the street in some tasty little joint where I rested my feet
and ate enchiladas with the most delectable sauce, and that liquor was liquid gold
and going down smooth.
So smooth and kissing my brain
I wondered that night if I might go insane.

Across the street the boys yelled, "Hey are you Kenny G? You fucking Kenny G?!"
I said, "No man, far from it, my friends. How about some of them two-for-ones?"
They entertained from the busy sidewalk in front of their cafe
with a skit they had worked up. A fast, hand-clapping pluck
like a percussive cupping that had a sound like slapping—
Clap, snap clappity smook, poppity clap, slap ploook
they tried to teach me, but I didn't have what it toook.

So off we ran to their bamboo hut
with a three-story bar on top of a private hang
where we drank, smoked funny weeds and sang.
Our faces loose, they began to flush
as white powders were laid down on the table. *Shush!*

Closing the blinds and closing the bar,
two of their señorita friends came with raven hair.
So beautiful in those lipstick-red huipiles—
I must have died and gone to the heavens.
Sexy as all that cocaine, MaryJane and tequila rained,
and wet we became.

After eating spicy chickens, we drove to nightclubs
where the girls got up and danced.
I stood near the speakers while the R&B, pop
split into my ears—

booosh, diggy-diggy-diggy, booosh, diggy-diggy
booosh, diggy-diggy-diggy boom.

Feeling so high, even this dark club seemed light and snowy,
(not a 95-degree den of human sweat and blow).

2.
I told them I had to split and catch the midnight bus to Mazatlan
where I was to meet a Russian friend of mine.

At the station the beautiful children approached me one after the other
selling Chiclets and little wooden turtles that bobbed their heads.
I couldn't resist buying a few dozen.
They were so proud to take my bits of money back to their mothers
where they too were waiting for the bus.
Happy mothers, smiling at me—
the children and mamas of Puerto Vallarteee!

On the bus por favor, it's time to take the black-night trip
skirting along steep mountain cliffs
around and up again on the rickety tank—
chugging through farmlands, stopping at slim-shady restrooms
where you might get shagged by the guy behind you on that bus of distrust.
Smoke that smoke, but keep close to that bus!
They just might leave you and then I would cuss
or surely perish at the hand of a thug
who stood in the shadows waiting to bug
    a gringo like me.

Back in my seat with the mothers and kids—
behind me a tuned-up, cracked-out crazy
cackling and laughing behind my head
    driving me nuts and to fear it spread.

Sociopathic sounds emitting from his mouth—
    a haunting, opiated tone.
His tripping, seething, breathing down my neck
surely he'd cut me or at least freak me out,
but if he touched me I'd smack him no doubt.
Ready to pounce and violently shout
and probably not survive the bout,
with this mental, gangrene gout.

Whatever floats your boat man...
Coconuts or mangoes.

3.
Many miles gone, I arrived in Mazatlan in a tired stupor
to meet my Russian friend, who I won't risk naming here.
We met back home in Minnesota the year before—

I taught her English, she made me clothes and taught me Russian.
She showed me art from Monet and Dali.
She made herbal remedies for my ailments of roots and spices.
We loved, we drank, traveled, and once we tripped on mushrooms
in New York somewhere in the Village.
We bought weed from cops
        and dwelled in the earthly shadows.

As I waited for my friend and lay in the hangover-healing sun,
I had a vision—
A great man appeared, surrounding a giant palm tree amidst a vast, blue sky—
A massive and clear projection of a GOD. He said, and I will always recall,
        What you did for the children was a very good thing.

After a few vaguely memorable but fun-filled hours,
I traveled further on sand-rolling caravans to foreign beaches.
I spoke with Vietnam vets who'd lived there since the war.
We drank and smoked and spoke.
I played mandolin and sang for people on the caravans
and the beautiful people clapped their hands.

4.
Morning came and I took the bus back to Puerto Vallarta to catch my flight.
I met up with my "Kenny G. friends" again, and whad'ya know...
The tequilla flowed,
        the pot growed,
                and the blow snowed.

We watched the sun come up and went to my pal's mother's house
where she cooked the most delicious, authentic Mexican breakfast I've ever had.
Beans and rice, eggs, mole sauce, and truthfully
I'm improvising the breakfast because I was too bamboozled to recall
exactly what that deliciousness was all about.

5.
All things fun and good (and bad),
must come to an end
so off to the airport
where I descended into an overblown, cocaine, pot, booze freak-out

so bad I had to approach a policía and ask for help.
I thought I was gonna die.
He laughed at me and said, "Amigo, you better sit down."
Then he left!

A young American girl walked past me and noticed my struggle.
She brought me a can of 7UP and asked if I was all right.
Then she left too!
I waited as discreetly as possible, near the departure gate.
I'm quite sure people were staring at me, thinking, *dude has had too much.*
The sugary-pop might have helped, or time.
I think
I slept
on the flight.

Home at last in Minneapolis, I entered the customs not-so-welcome area
where the agent asked for my ID
I flipped open my wallet and in a split-second stroke of luck
looked down to notice a small bag of white powder hanging out for all to see,
except the agent hadn't looked down before I could snap it shut, pull it off the counter
and pull my ID out in seclusion.

I think I may have killed an angel—
(again).

Breathing a shallow sigh of relief, I turned toward the luggage belt
where another customs agent walked her German shepherd around.
Visions of iron bars, thick beads of sweat flew off my forehead,
YET GOD IS HERE!
And he's left a garbage can perfectly positioned for me to dispose of said cokey bag
before ole Shep' came sniffin' around.

Retrieved my bag.
Caught a cab.
Arrived home.
Went to bed.

Scottie Miller

Born in Minneapolis, Scottie Miller began piano lessons at age six, the start of a long and vibrant career in music and the arts. He is first and foremost a pianist and songwriter. He is best known in the blues and roots realm, though he marches bravely through everything from jazz to rock, classical to Americana, gospel to funk. He's always had a natural affinity for New Orleans music. "His playing is swampy and soulful, and his voice boasts grit and firewater." (Rick Mason, *City Pages*)

From a lifetime spent on the road, on the stage and in the recording studio, his lyrics convey a cathartic approach to writing. "If you can tell me how you do it, maybe I can find a better way to cope."

Scottie has toured with Rock & Roll Hall of Fame legend Bo Diddley, has been published by Hal Leonard, has been inducted three times into the Minnesota Blues Hall of Fame and has released 11 self-produced albums. He leads the Scottie Miller Band and tours with four-time Grammy-nominated singer Ruthie Foster. They have appeared at iconic venues such as Carnegie Hall and Austin City Limits. He penned the song "I Was Called" (cowritten with Foster) on the album *Almost Home*, by six-time Grammy Award–winning gospel group the Blind Boys of Alabama.

His poetry ability was nurtured by his literature teacher during his time attending Berklee College of Music in 1986 and has been hidden like buried diamonds beneath his song lyrics over the years. Scottie chose these selections himself, and this collection reveals a lifetime of imagery through his own kaleidoscopic view.

Scottie was inspired to improvise on the piano while he recited these poems, allowing the words to shape the music organically. The result is contained on the triumphant album version of *Carnival Cocoon*, which features 23 poems from this book set to his original music. He conveys his spoken and sung word with jazz beat, folk and blues composition while lush, classically tinged string quintet arrangements surround his shining piano and vocals.

Scottie is an active, passionate member of the Twin Cities recovery community. He works with other recovering addicts and alcoholics, and shares his experience, strength and hope through his music, poetry and live performance.

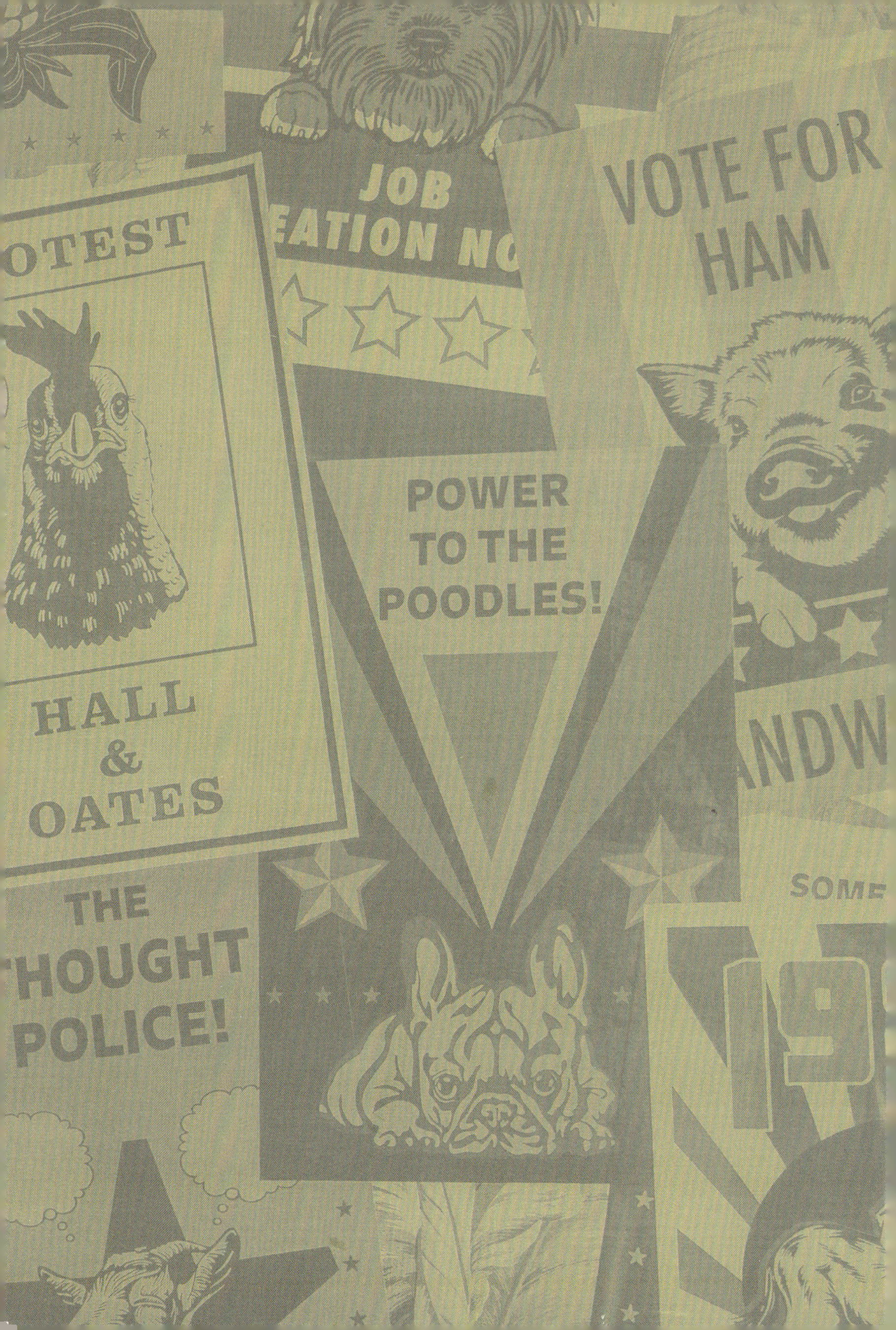

JOB
EATION NO
VOTE FOR
HAM
OTEST
POWER
TO THE
POODLES!
HALL
&
OATES
ANDW
THE
HOUGHT
POLICE!
SOME